Here is the Nativity Story, traditionally illustrated and carefully retold for young readers and listeners.

British Library Cataloguing in Publication Data

Hately, David
  Baby Jesus.
  1. Jesus Christ. Nativity
  I. Title   II. Rotheroe, Christopher   III. Series
  232.921
  ISBN 0-7214-1313-7

First edition

Published by Ladybird Books Ltd Loughborough Leicestershire UK
Ladybird Books Inc Auburn Maine 04210 USA

Printed in England (3)

Baby Jesus

written by DAVID HATELY
illustrated by CHRIS ROTHEROE

Ladybird Books

In the little town of Nazareth there lived a girl called Mary.

When she was old enough to marry, a carpenter named Joseph asked her to be his wife.

Mary was happy, because she loved
Joseph. Soon she was busy getting
everything ready for the wedding.

But God had something even more
important for Mary to do.

5

God sent his angel, Gabriel, to visit Mary in Nazareth.

"God loves you and wants you to help him," he told her.

At first, Mary was frightened.

But Gabriel said, "Don't be afraid. God wants you to be the mother of his child, his son. When the baby is born you must call him Jesus."

The name Jesus means *Saviour*.

Augustus wanted to find out how many people lived in that part of his empire. He commanded every man to return to the town of his birth to sign a special register of names.

Joseph's family came from the town of Bethlehem. It was a long way from Nazareth. Joseph had to walk there, while Mary rode beside him on a donkey.

All the inns of Bethlehem were full, so Joseph did his best to make Mary comfortable in a stable. At least it was warm, with plenty of clean straw to lie on.

And there Mary gave birth to her baby son.

There was no cot for him. So Mary wrapped God's son in a shawl and laid him in a manger.

That night, in the fields outside Bethlehem, some shepherds were keeping watch over their flocks in case there were any wild animals on the prowl.

As the shepherds sat by their fire, the angel Gabriel appeared to them. The fields shone with the light of God.

At first, the shepherds were frightened.

But Gabriel said, "Don't be afraid! I have great news for you, which you must share with everyone else. Today, God's son has been born in Bethlehem. God is with you, here on Earth! Go and see him – he's not in a palace, he's wrapped in a shawl lying in a manger."

When Gabriel had finished
speaking, the skies above him filled
with a great choir of angels.

Glory to God in heaven, they sang.
*Peace to all the men and women —
and the children, too — who are
friends with God.*

The shepherds hurried away to
Bethlehem, telling everyone they
met about the angel's message.

The shepherds found the stable
where the new-born baby was lying
in Mary's arms.

Mary listened quietly to their story,
treasuring their words.

And when the shepherds left the
stable they shouted for joy. Like the
angels, they sang *Glory to God!*

For everything had turned out just
as Gabriel said it would.

Mary and Joseph called the baby
Jesus – the name that Gabriel had
given him before his birth.

As Mary looked at Jesus she was
glad that she had been chosen to
have God's son.

Far away, in a land towards the east, some wise men saw a new star rising in the night sky.

Because of their great learning, they knew why the star had appeared. It was a sign that a king had just been born in King Herod's lands.

The wise men immediately set out on a long journey to the city of Jerusalem.

They expected to find the new-born king there, living in Herod's palace.

But there was no baby prince in
King Herod's palace.

"Where is he?" the wise men asked
Herod. "We saw his star rising! We
want to visit him."

Herod, too, wanted to know where
he could find the new-born king
whose star had appeared in the skies.

He wanted to kill him.

He was afraid that the child would
one day take away his crown.

King Herod sent for his advisers
and asked them if they could help
the wise men to find the new-born
king.

They answered, "It was foretold:
*Out of Bethlehem will come a
leader. He will be a shepherd to the
people.*"

28

Herod turned to the wise men.

"Go to Bethlehem," he said.
"When you have found the child,
come back and let me know where
he is. I, too, would like to visit
him."

The wise men set out from Herod's
palace, and there in front of them
was the star. The sight of it filled
them with joy.

The star moved ahead of them,
leading them to Bethlehem, and
stopped above the place where
Jesus lay.

Going inside, the wise men saw
baby Jesus lying in the manger
and at once they fell to their knees.

The wise men opened their treasures and gave Jesus three special gifts.

They gave him gold because that is the sign of a king, and Jesus was the King of Heaven.

They gave him sweet-smelling frankincense because that is the sign of God's presence, and Jesus was God's son.

They gave him bitter myrrh because that is the sign of suffering, and Jesus was to die on the Cross.

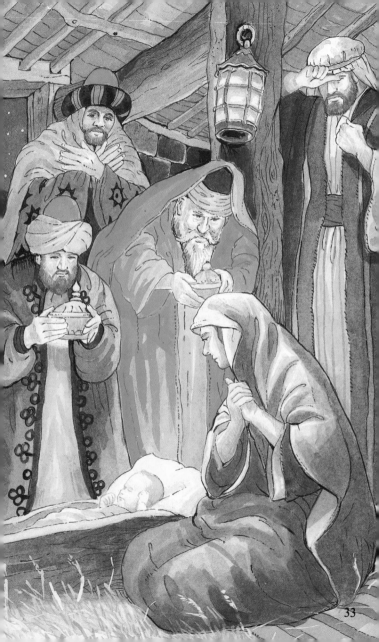

The wise men intended to return to Jerusalem so that they could tell King Herod about Jesus.

But God's angel came to them in a dream.

"Go home by a different way!" said Gabriel. "Stay away from King Herod. He means to harm Jesus."

So the wise men didn't go back to tell King Herod about Jesus. They left Bethlehem secretly and returned to their own country by a different way.

God knew that Jesus was still in
danger, so he sent his angel to visit
Joseph.

"Herod is going to kill Jesus,"
Gabriel said. "Take the child and

his mother into Egypt. Stay there until I tell you that it's safe to return.''

That night, Joseph set out with Mary and the baby Jesus, heading for safety in the land of Egypt.

Herod flew into a rage when he realised that the wise men were not coming back to see him.

He didn't know exactly when the infant king had been born, so he ordered his soldiers to go to Bethlehem and kill every boy under the age of two.

Herod had no idea that Jesus had already left Bethlehem and was safe in the land of Egypt.

Not long afterwards, King Herod died. Once more God's angel appeared to Joseph.

"Get up!" said Gabriel. "Go back to your own land. Herod is dead! Jesus is no longer in danger."

So the little family made another long journey, but this time they were happy because at last they were going home.

Mary and Joseph settled down in their home at Nazareth, where Jesus grew up wise and strong, loved by everyone who knew him.

He did everything that Mary and Joseph asked.

But Mary remembered the angel's words. *God wants you to be the mother of his child, his son.*

She knew that one day it would be time for Jesus to begin his Father's work.